L.I.S.T.E.N.

L.I.S.T.E.N.

Ellie Van Arsdale

BALBOA.
PRESS

A DIVISION OF HAY HOUSE

Balboa Press books may be ordered through booksellers or by contacting:

Balboa Press
A Division of Hay House
1663 Liberty Drive
Bloomington, IN 47403
www.balboapress.com
1-(877) 407-4847

Because of the dynamic nature of the Internet, any web addresses or
links contained in this book may have changed since publication and
may no longer be valid. The views expressed in this work are solely those
of the author and do not necessarily reflect the views of the publisher,
and the publisher hereby disclaims any responsibility for them.

The author of this book does not dispense medical advice or prescribe the use
of any technique as a form of treatment for physical, emotional, or medical
problems without the advice of a physician, either directly or indirectly. The
intent of the author is only to offer information of a general nature to help
you in your quest for emotional and spiritual well-being. In the event you use
any of the information in this book for yourself, which is your constitutional
right, the author and the publisher assume no responsibility for your actions.

Any people depicted in stock imagery provided by Thinkstock are models,
and such images are being used for illustrative purposes only.
Certain stock imagery © Thinkstock.

ISBN: 978-1-4525-4918-7 (sc)
ISBN: 978-1-4525-4917-0 (e)

Library of Congress Control Number: 2012904922
Printed in the United States of America
Balboa Press rev. date:6/12/2012

DEDICATION

This book is dedicated to my
Aunt Lydia
Who showed me inner strength
And unconditional love.

INTRODUCTION

Receiving an idea and a supportive direction to write a book of my own, germinated in my intuitive thinking, several years ago. The inner whispers I heard encouraged me to one day create a manuscript that could help others as I was learning to help myself. The idea and the intention to share what I was learning about spiritual enlightenment and positive living took root, in love, within my heart. Forgiveness, letting go, accepting change and changing myself were subjects that required healing, growth, and understanding in my life.

As years sped by way too quickly, I chose and read many excellent, well-written words by inspirational and educated authors. I bought 5 x 8 lined index cards and put the title and author of each book I was studying, at the top of each card. On each card, I wrote the significant messages that were teaching me in significant, positive ways. Everywhere I went, I took my cards and when I stopped to take a break, I read the cards over for increased clarity and inner exploration. The books added up as did the years. It wasn't long before I realized that I was accepting many of the messages of wisdom that I had been studying. I began changing my own vocabulary, attitude, and behavior. As I changed my thinking, I changed and purposely, became a new Ellie. I felt my growth and welcomed the healing into my being, accepting each arriving gift, with thanksgiving.

Last year, the seed that had germinated and taken root in my intuitive thinking, years ago, began to grow and blossom, urgently requesting, a chance to reach full bloom. I started this manuscript and am eternally grateful that I am now bringing it to you to read with the intention that you might find it beneficial and inspirational for your life, that you might choose to begin a new personal journey for yourself.

Thank you for giving me the opportunity to share what I have learned so far with you. It is a continuing educational process that brings me new truths and everlasting trust in God every day. I especially, want to thank Ronald Gillmeister for his enthusiastic, positive and loving support and Melissa Kushnaryov for her kind and loving assistance in solving my computer dilemmas.

Ellie Van Arsdale

Every second of every minute of every twenty four hour day that you live in this world is a second that is giving you life. Every precious breath emanating from your lungs is bringing you the gift of love beyond measure. Each one is providing you with an amazing opportunity to live your days with increased awareness of your individual path and partnership with God. Each one is gifting you with a positive affirmation to love yourself, to know yourself, and to reach out to the world in which you live in accepting, compassionate ways. If you are willing to see your breaths as tiny miracles of enlightenment, you will find strength and guidance in each breath as you courageously take action to move forward in your life. Let your inner self teach you enlightenment and newness. L.I.S.T.E.N. It takes only one breath to voice the affirmation, "I am loved beyond measure."

Open my eyes that I may see. Glimpses of truth Thou hast for me
Place in my hands the wonderful key That shall unclasp and set me free
Open my ears that I may hear. Voices of truth Thou sendest clear And
While the wave notes fall on my ear, Everything false will disappear
Open my mouth, and let me bear. Gladly the warm truth everywhere
Open my heart and let me prepare. Love with Thy children thus to share.
Silently now I wait for Thee. Ready my God, Thy will to see
Open my eyes, my ears, my heart, illumine me, Spirit divine!

Christian Hymn from Psalm 119:18
H. Scott 1895
Clara H. Scott 1895

It does not matter who you are, where you are, or what life has brought to you in this present moment of your journey. Forgiveness and a loving willingness to move on to a

1

happier, healthier world for yourself is a decision only you can make. Finding your way to positive change with a knowing and a trust you are being led to new truths and increased awareness, is the result of your decision to have the courage to look within and do your necessary work.

Each of us has a difficult journey. Not one of us is exempt. You will never get it all accomplished. In the final realization of what life is all about, this is okay! Continuing to plan and to dream keeps you positive, active and brings joy into your life. Your willingness to begin a new journey for yourself, and to emerge with a more mature awareness, and a new compassion for yourself and the world in which you live, is the first step in releasing blame of others, and blame of God. L. I. S. T. E. N. Let your inner self teach you enlightenment and newness.

"There is growing quality in everything; thus we all go on our way, different in many experiences, common enough in others, to make us all children of one plan, which most of us come to see is divine. Whether we laugh or cry as we come to the light and dark places, those of us who do recognize divinity in our lives, go forward with praise and thanksgiving."

Abbie May Palmer
1929

Willingness to enter the black, starless nights of our inner selves is scary. It takes our trust, our time, our courage, and most importantly, our faith. It is true that no one can fully understand what you are going through or how you are managing to live it all out. No one sees inside you, no one feels what you are experiencing emotionally, physically or spiritually. No one sees how you are coping, how you are getting through this day. Perhaps no friend or family member knows how desperately you want out of a relationship, out of your loneliness, out of your chronic pain, or out of your financial catastrophe.

Our negative thoughts often pop up unexpectedly shocking us and others. They act as astonishing wake up calls for us to see the reality of our behavior. They show us how we are expressing our despair, and our anger with our negative actions. Strong responses to our bad behavior from those we know and from strangers, can be gifts of new knowledge, if we are not defensive, and think we are always right. In order to recognize the positive in us, it is necessary for us to see the negative. It is only in seeing both that we can make a conscious decision to be more positive, more loving, more accepting, The gift is in accepting both sides, in owning both sides. We cannot see our beautiful aurora borealis lights until we have experienced our dark, starless nights. Give yourself permission to hear without judgment. As my mother has written, "recognize divinity" in your life and move forward "with praise and thanksgiving." Affirm this knowledge and accept its healing presence. L.I.S.T.E.N. Let your inner self teach you enlightenment and newness.

What are you hearing now? What has been unheard until now that is re-emerging stronger and clearer than ever before? Is there a new song? Hear its loving message surrounding you with new hope and a new dream. Open your mind and your heart to the music playing for your ears only. Tune to the channel that is coming loud and clear with positive lyrics of love beyond measure. Re-affirm to yourself that you are listening and providing for yourself, that you are taking action, being nurturing and re-storing your spirit. Trust your music. Listen to its vibrant melodies and affirmative words for new and better days. See the positive messages that are everywhere, not only in song. Welcome the new discoveries you are hearing, seeing, feeling. They are here to help you help yourself.

You might decide to create mantras of your own making. Select a song, a quotation, a phrase, a picture, a scene from nature that speaks to your ears alone and brings comfort and joy to you. For instance, take a word that means something to you and make an acronym with it. Here is S.T.O.P.:

Stay
True to my
Own
Peace

I like the word smile because I want to do a lot more of it! Here is another meaningful acronym that I have made for myself from S.M.I.L.E.

See
Messages of
Inspiration and
Love
Everywhere

You might want to write a haiku of five lines which has the formula of: line 1: 5 syllables line 2: 7 syllables line 3: 5 syllables line 4: 7 syllables line 5: 7 syllables. A haiku that brings meaning to me is:

My heart is a well,
Never dry, but sometimes low.
Come rain and fill it.
To joy overflowing so
Laughter and peace reign again

My mother loved to write poetry and I have kept her words as inspiration for my own writing. She wrote this about breathing:

In the trees, shrubs, everywhere
The birds are singing songs
That vary in tone, length, and rhythm
All of them so full of the joy of living
That I lift up to Heaven
Eyes filled with gratitude
For my joy of hearing music
That environs me like the air I breathe

Abbie May Palmer
1930

You are creative, and can choose what makes you happy; just start doing it. Whatever you choose to create will be yours alone and will bring special recognition to your days. Try it, it is fun. It keeps the mind active, positive, and loving.

In addition to writing your words, also sing with them, dance with them, paint with them. etc. and connect with their positive, loving messages. Feel new inspiration as you detach from your negative voices. Know that you are being heard and that from your intuition, the answers will be yours to live with new maturity and wisdom, when you are ready to receive them.

In your living space, you might want to give yourself a wrap around hug. I've done that for years every place I have lived. I have placed plants, pictures, travel treasures, etc., objects of all sizes that bring meaning and contentment to me around the room. When I am home and living in each room, it feels like a wrap around hug that makes me feel safe and loved.

Nothing has to be costly or expansive. What is important and what works, is that your home brings you a warm, cozy feeling and a calming atmosphere. My home, whether it has been a studio room, an apartment or a house, is my retreat. When I walk in my front door, I feel thankfulness for the space that shelters and nurtures me.

The answers we seek so desperately can never be rushed and seem to arrive one at a time, often unexpectedly. They arrive as truth, filling us with a new understanding, a new compassion, a new clarity. In the interim, continue your journey, continue your study, continue to trust in the Divine. One day, seemingly, out of the blue, you will get it. Your answer will be there for you, has always been there for you, but finally, you have been prepared to receive it! Listen to the positive change in your attitude, to the gratitude of new discovery in self. You are never alone even when you think you are.

Believe you have what you need at the time you need it. Believe, trust, and most importantly, be brave enough to go inside yourself to ask your questions and give praise for the wisdom you are receiving. You are loved beyond measure.

My husband and I married five days after he graduated from college. He had been in the Army during the Korean War and had finished college on the GI Bill. After college, he accepted a position with a national telephone company that would teach him the business from the ground up. He began by following telephone line gangs throughout the country and digging the ditches for the telephone poles. I had been a scholarship student and completed two years of college before we married.

After purchasing a mobile home, moving every two years, becoming parents to two beautiful sons, we finally found ourselves in a permanent location, buying our first house after six years of marriage. Nine months after moving to our new home, my husband was hospitalized with severe, acute pancreatitis. When I was told he had a 50-50 chance of living, I put his health on the up side of his making it, and staying with us. I refused to accept what the doctors were telling me between the lines.

Not knowing the end was so close, but feeling an urgency to take the boys to the hospital, I dressed our sons in their

Easter outfits on Good Friday and took them on a surprise visit to see their father in the hospital. The nurses and I were not certain if we could lift him into a wheelchair, but luckily, we did it. In nine weeks he had lost fifty pounds and was so frail that I worried what reaction the boys would have to him.

There was no need to be concerned. When I wheeled him out to the reception room, other people gasped, but the boys embraced him. This was their daddy. The older boy said, "Daddy, you're not wearing your glasses." That was the only change he saw. His father smiled a wonderful, loving smile and tried to hug them both. Everyone who heard the statement was touched by our son's words of love. That sentence spoken by my not quite five year old son on Good Friday remains one of the most loving and beautiful sentences I have ever heard.

Early on Palm Sunday morning, he passed away. I was with him and although he was in a coma, I hope he felt my hand touching his, and heard me tell him how much I loved him, how much I wanted him to stay. Almost a week later, he was given a military ceremony and buried at the top of a lovely hill under a beautiful, maple tree in Arlington National Cemetery. Following the military ceremony my mother-in-law, a close friend whose husband had married us, my mother, my husband's boss and his wife, and our sons grieved with me in our home as we shared happy stories about his life.

Two days following the funeral I found myself alone with my sons. Everyone had returned home to Florida and it was assumed that we would follow in the near future. Because I had no siblings, no other family except my mother, it seemed inevitable that I would decide to move back to Florida in due time. I was told that was where we needed to be.

After six years in a small 8 wide, 35 foot mobile home, we had moved to a house with a yard in a beautiful neighborhood and within walking distance to excellent schools, our church, and a good shopping area. We were happy and felt this was where we belonged. This was where we would build our future. Even though I understood nothing, and felt everything, the answer was intuitively loud and clear to me. The boys and I would stay in Arlington, Virginia.

There were countless unanswered questions. What would I do, how could I keep the house, the car, bring clothing and food and emotional loving sustenance to my precious sons? I asked my questions in faith with no answers forthcoming immediately.

One night, soon after the funeral, after reading the boys a story and hearing their prayers, suicidal thoughts suddenly engulfed me and within minutes, had drowned all my hope. As I rose to enter the bathroom, a sudden and immense wave of overpowering love, stopped me and I could not move. Breaking through my bereavement, dislodging all barriers of despair, a voice whispered in my ear, "It's not time, you're needed here." Tears of guilt exploded. Fortunately, there would have been nothing to take in the medicine cabinet. When I could not sleep for much of those nine weeks, I had asked for something to take to help me sleep. However, the doctor denied my request. He told me that he and the nurses had observed me, thought I would make an excellent nurse, and felt that I had the strength to face whatever happened, on my own. This statement of confidence strengthened me, and helped me to know that I could do it, with God's help.

The first long cry alone since my husband's death took precedence over sleep that night. In the days that followed, the tears flowed just as freely every night, but I had begun to depend upon that inner whisper. How could I want to take my own life when my two young sons whom I loved and adored were sleeping in the next room? I wanted to love them and guide them, I wanted to see them grow into fine men, I wanted to share with them every step of our journey together.

Oh God, if ever I am to become what I want to become
Help me now.

Fear has tiptoed into my mind and stolen my reconciled
thoughts
Decision has turned to negative thinking
Confusion engulfs my being
Hope seems distant
And despair too near

Oh God, if ever I am to become what I want to become
Help me now
My soul lies dormant remembering past joys
My mind takes shelter in what was
Help me now to awaken lost hope
And trust all to Thee.

Eleanor Van Arsdale

In my intense moments of desperation, God lovingly taught me that I was not alone, had never been alone, and would never again feel spiritually alone, unloved, unguided. I had felt His love surrounding me and enveloping me with new hope. In the years that have followed living out my life, even in times of despair, illness, betrayal, abandonment, and physical loneliness, I have never felt spiritually alone. From that moment after Al's death to this moment, I still know and feel God's love for me. Even though my personal journey has dramatically changed in the years that have followed, God's blessed assurance to me that night continues to be my pilot light for strength and courage. With a willingness I had never known before, I started to hear, to see with an open heart and a knowing inside of me that I was safe, regardless. I became willing to venture down a new path to forgive myself and to forgive God.

Every day it seemed I searched for answers and none were there for me. One night, again unable to sleep with my worries, I felt a presence in my bedroom that permeated the entire room. The air was thick, someone was there. Intuitively, I knew that the God who had told me "Ellie, you're needed here" was in my bedroom proving to me that I most certainly was not alone. I became so scared that I jumped up from my bed, ran into the bathroom across the hall, turned on the light, and immediately felt shame! God had come to me again, and I was not welcoming. Where was my faith, where was my trust, where was my courage? I was all bluff; I had no courage.

I have never felt remorse as much as I did that night in that bathroom with the light on. I turned off the light, and returned to bed beating myself up for being so stupid and fearful! I started to pray and I remember saying, "Please forgive me, I know it was you. I just got so scared. I know you came because I am so alone, feel no support, and am facing everything without knowing any answers. I was feeling so abandoned when you came to reassure me! Please come back again, please come soon. I promise I won't be scared. I will just lie here and thank you for loving me. I promise to trust that if You have something I need to know, you will tell me and I will hear it. And if you don't say anything, I will just know that you love me and You are here to give me the reassurance that I am never alone." Believe me when I tell you, I felt I had really blown it and wondered if God would ever return. It helped to write these words:

> For all the moments in my day
> When thoughts are inconsistent and confusing
> Help me, Lord, to learn patience
> Give me the courage to stay positive
> Guide me to restore the vitality I have lost.

I waited and waited and waited. Every night I went to bed saying it would be okay for me to just lie in my bed and not feel any fear, if and when God came back to my room.

I decided I would feel thankfulness that God loved me so much he forgave me and chose to return with the same message. Just when I thought it might never really happen, it happened! One evening I had already been asleep when something awakened me suddenly and I felt the same presence, the same thickness of air in the room I had felt weeks before. This time I kept my promise and did not panic. I remember vividly saying, "Thank you for coming. Even though my heart is pounding fast, I know that you are here to show me that you love me and are always with me."

The room stayed thick with God's presence, but I closed my eyes feeling love all around me, love I did not understand, and had never known before, in such a wonderful way! I don't recall going to sleep that night because it just happened.

"Enter into His gates with thanksgiving, And into His Courts with praise, Be thankful unto Him and bless His name."

Psalm 100:4
Holy Bible
New King James Version

It seemed almost immediately after my husband's death, and most certainly, after everyone had left after the funeral to return home, I felt an overwhelming, intense realization that it would just be me now that would have to provide in every area for my two sons. This, amazingly, never felt like a burden or a fear to me. Although it was solely up to me for our livelihood, I always thought we would make it. The mortgage payments, the food, clothing, medical and dental expenses, transportation, education, entertainment, gas, etc. were all challenges and not obstacles. For some reason, I had no doubt in my mind that we would make it and make it together really well!

How did I feel that way? I remember feeling a definite assurance that my husband had trusted me to do what I would need to do to raise his sons. We had no savings, and although the mortgage payment was paid for the current month, the checking account balance was diminishing quickly. I had lost my beloved husband, but in his leaving me, he had bequeathed to me, the best of himself. And he trusted the best in me. I took this information very seriously and through prayer and trust in God, I began slowly to put into action a dream and a plan for our future as a family. My strength came from the blessed assurance I was hearing and feeling so strongly during that difficult time; I was not alone!

Joe Crocker sings, "God, lift me up where I belong," My prayer became, "Please God, lift me up where I belong." The one thing I knew for certain is that I had a strong determination to raise my two boys in a loving, positive, safe atmosphere, to teach them to think independently and to give them the confidence that I trusted them. How God was going to help me accomplish this, I had no idea. I only knew that I could not show trusting unless I trusted. And I did. The love and the message I had so strongly felt and heard in my bedroom returned to me often, and paved our way to a new life.

Believe you have what you need to have at the time you need it. In the following weeks and months that first year of widowhood, the answers that I prayed for came in surprising ways. My husband's company, knowing I had no money and no other steady means of financial support, gave me one year of my husband's salary.

I opened a checking account and a savings account at a local bank. I put some of the money in the savings account and marked it for education, the rest in the checking account for future incoming bills, and for bills currently owed. I applied for and received a credit card to utilize for emergencies and to travel home for Christmas vacation. I interviewed and was hired as a part time sales associate at a women's dress shop in the local nearby mall. Fortunately, I had an understanding woman boss who allowed me to work irregular hours and to bring a sandwich with me.

We shopped the sales at JC Penney's and tried to stick to the budget I made out the beginning of every month. We ate more economical meals and shared frozen chicken and turkey pot pie dinners, hamburgers, hamburger casseroles, macaroni and cheese, chicken every way I could fix it, tater tots, and fish sticks. We attended pot luck dinners at church and treated ourselves to Mac Donald's on special occasions! We were making it!!! Within months the Social Security check for the boys began to arrive at the same time every month. The following summer I was in good enough shape to join the neighborhood pool association and to give the boys swimming lessons there.

In the next two years I bought an organ on time and gave the boys music lessons. I picked a small Hammond organ because it had all the fun stops like trumpets, clarinet, drums, etc. that boys really like and I thought maybe, just maybe, they would enjoy learning how to play, if I provided an instrument that kept their attention. Kent excelled in his swimming and Mark excelled in his music, later studying classical guitar.

We attended our local church on a regular basis and became very active in several of their family activities. Our minister and his wife had three children of their own and began asking us to their home to share celebrations with them. The boys and I made friends with other members of the church who had children the same age and often visited them. We soon discovered we had an extended family.

Often on Sunday afternoon after attending church, having lunch, and taking a nap, we would get in the car and go for a Sunday drive with no specific destination in mind. This drive became a fun game for us that I have always called, "Let's get Mommy lost!" Since I have no sense of direction, this was a cinch to do! I would just drive turning left here, making a right there, going straight until I would announce, "I'm lost!" I'd hear, "No, Mommy, we're not lost. Just go left for two blocks, then straight for six, and we'll be on our way home." I'd say, "No, I think maybe we should just turn around right here." But then I'd get loud " No's" and a " Stay on this street!" We had a lot of fun bantering and teasing each other with this game.

However, there were instances where nothing worked, and we'd just keep on being lost. I'd say at that point, "We are really lost today." And I'd get back, "Mommy, we're not THAT far away from home." Eventually we would find our path back to our area. If I had enough money to stop at our local ice cream shop for an ice cream cone, we would stop. If not, we'd drive home and have our treat there. It was always a very happy day for me when I could surprise the boys and say, "Let's stop and get a double dip ice cream cone today!"

Once I had put us on a budget, and found a part-time job, I filled out an application for entrance to two nearby colleges in Washington, DC and had copies of my previous college transcripts sent to each college. In the mail one day, I received a letter that all of my previous scholarship credits from Emerson College in Boston were accepted by both American University and George Washington University in Washington, DC. The following fall semester I entered American University as a BA degree candidate with a double major in English and in Speech.

Two weeks before beginning classes at American University, all leads for a baby sitter had dwindled to nothing. Then, one evening, a face and the name Freda focused before me and I sensed an urgent request to "call her to care for the boys." I had seen this woman in church and only knew she had recently arrived from Canada. I had met her briefly during coffee hour following church. I called a church acquaintance and Freda's full name and telephone number were immediately supplied.

I was astonished when I called Freda describing the hours I would need a baby sitter while I attended classes in Washington. I did not know her, in fact, no one knew her well, and here I was trusting she could help me, not knowing what her credentials were. When she said she would be happy to help me, she asked me who had recommended her, and told me that she wasn't aware that anyone at the church knew she had been a social worker in Canada. She explained to me that her job had been to place children whose mothers had to work or go back to school in good home environments. Freda's professional experience created a normal home atmosphere and positive, loving discipline for my two little boys. God's divine guidance had led her to me.

There were other problems such as changing my younger son's school and the worry of his hospitalization at mid-term time with pneumonia. When he was admitted, we were taken to the pediatric ward. As soon as Mark entered the room he noticed that one of the other little boys was holding a large, stuffed green snake about six feet long. He told me immediately, "Mama, I want one of those." I replied, "Okay, honey, I'll go out and get you one and bring it back for you.."

Little did I know that long six foot stuffed snakes were currently the most popular toy for children. I thought I could easily find one in the first toy department I drove to, but no such luck. I drove from store to store leaving our regular shopping areas and trying new stores that were farther out. One store told me, "Sorry, you're a few minutes late. Our last snake just left the store." The afternoon sped on and I still had no snake. My son, a little over four years old, was in the hospital with pneumonia. I could not enter his hospital room empty handed. I had to have a large six foot stuffed snake in my arms. I was Mama and I was supposed to have an easy time getting his needs met. I kept moving on determined to find a snake and was pretty much in panic mode when I found an out of the way store a long way from the hospital. There, in a big box at the back of the store, was one gorgeous, bright yellow, happy, six foot stuffed snake lying all alone, just waiting for me, to come and buy him! How lucky! I felt as if I had won the lottery for Mark!

I drove back to the hospital and when my son saw me enter his room with the very long six foot bright yellow stuffed snake in my arms, his face lit up. He eagerly reached up to hold it. His excited smile, upon receiving it, WAS winning the lottery! His smile that day in that hospital in Arlington, Virginia remains one of the happiest smiles I have ever received.

I stayed with Mark the rest of the day then went home to be with Kent. That night the resident pediatric doctor put Mark on his shoulders and took him on his rounds. Mark was well enough to go home in two days. He recovered quickly and not for one minute for many days to come was he without his happy, six foot yellow snake. I had no time to study or prepare for mid-term exams that year. I was encouraged to take them anyway and thankfully passed them all.

Writing at that time began to fill a void for me. It felt good to put my feelings and my thoughts on paper. The writing started me on a life long journey to help myself so I could help others. And I had two little boys who required a healthy, positive mother.

The Lord will provide
Know this, it is freeing you
Cast out fear for fear is not of His making
What do you fear? The unknown future that is not yours to see?
Stay anchored to Him... stay and hold on... Fight the negative
Be willing to trust, be willing to listen, be willing to learn.

Eleanor Van Arsdale

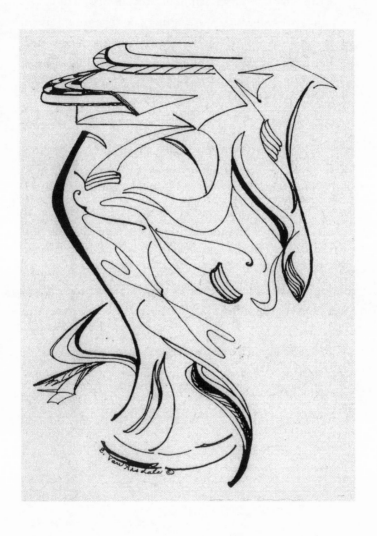

Please take time for prayer, for quiet time alone to meditate, to listen and reflect with an open heart every day. Take time to express yourself in healthy, positive ways.

Your willingness to say a loving goodbye to outgrown needs and ideas and to voice a welcoming hello to new ideas and needs that require your attention and active participation helps you to truly feel and see how you have arrived where you are today.

Become aware of your own participation in life and look at that participation without judging it. You have a responsibility to yourself to admit your own shortcomings and to see them differently, to see your active part in every episode you are living. You can start today to send love and forgiveness to your past and the painful situations you have allowed to live in your heart and in your body for too long a time. God is providing you with the strength and the courage to release your long held pain and to let it go. Most importantly, the realization that past hurts and painful situations have been carried by your body and your mind, birth healthy intentions and positive results. Every one of us has experienced and lived deep hurt and everyone one of us deserves compassion and forgiveness.

Through the Storms

I am walking in a bitter cold snowstorm of sadness
The freezing wind swirls around me penetrating deep inside
Its toxic velocity has arrived out of nowhere, surprisingly vicious
Invading my tranquility, threatening my well being
Its unstoppable force moves without warning into an angry, torrential
rain
I hear my heavy heart cry out loud staccatos of sobbing
And hear my sobs become a volatile hurricane
Intuitively, I allow this unstoppable force to complete its journey
Knowing I cannot go on until it has been allowed full disclosure.

The sobbing ends. Only quiet tears remain.
Silence inhabits my atmosphere
I welcome the calming solitude and sense disclosure imminent
Within the stillness, it comes softly, telling me to let go of the hurt
To release and detach from it with love
To forgive myself, to see a clearer vision of my purpose here
I feel the truth in the wisdom of these words and realize with
Thankfulness I am moving to a better place
The storms that penetrated my heart so deeply are gifting me
With definitive insight
Stronger and wiser, I choose to detach, to forgive with love
And move forward
To change myself.

Eleanor Van Arsdale

To forgive and move on with a stronger determination to change yourself for the better is a responsible, courageous, positive act of faith. It is a prayer for a healthy new beginning and a willingness to trust the truth that is awakening in your spirit with definitive insight. It is a decision to love yourself and others without measure.

Your life is moving forward and although you have unanswered questions, your spirit through your willingness to change yourself, is showing you how to do it. It is a huge endeavor to face what we would prefer not to look at ever, but truth and knowing set us free to love ourselves and to love others, unconditionally. It becomes, then, not an endeavor, but a blessing we feel excited about receiving.

Taking the time for reflection, meditation, and prayer help me to grow and discover when it is time to let hurtful scenarios no longer take space in my inner world and home. I understand them better now and try with prayer, meditation, and affirmations to let them go. Seems though, that new ones to tackle keep entering my mind, and often old ones stay around too long. And the tears just appear. For me, in the morning upon awakening, I sometimes feel a tear. At first, I was startled to open my eyes, and feel the wet warmth of moisture gathering its momentum. The tears seem, always, to remind me of the gift of Truth I am being given They come abruptly and either come daily for only a second or two or do not return for a long time.

The Return

It is morning,
I have awakened to a new day
My heart is filled with gratitude.

In the corner of each eye, I feel moisture gathering strength
A single trickle of wet mobility soon begins to gently caress
Each cheek as it travels in a familiar path
Stopping at my chin.

The tears of thankfulness have returned
Reminding me of God's grace
Alerting my Spirit to the truth of God's love
That I am never alone
That each morning is a gift, a new beginning.

It is morning.
I have awakened to a new day
My heart has voiced its gratitude.

Eleanor Van Arsdale

Meditating, reading, seeking help from a counselor, saying affirmations, continuing to study, to journal, to review and to release has helped me see the purpose of my own life. When you make a decision to go back and relive something that you felt hurt you deeply, your willingness to see the gift it holds for you will be life changing. The old scenarios return, but this time, you view them as events in your life that have made you who you are today. The old negative feelings are replaced with a new compassion and an enlightened willingness to forgive yourself and others. You begin to see how you are actively participating in every event, how you have changed and are continuing to change.

Meditating, just sitting quietly alone in an atmosphere of safety with no set intention, is freeing and calming. It can be done for any length of time, and can truly make a difference in the way you look at everything. Try to be very kind, very sweet to yourself and make it a new habit in your daily activities.

Be steadfast and gentle in thought.

Abbie May Palmer
1929

Scheduling time to meditate helps me accept and listen to myself with a clearer awareness of my feelings and beliefs. I have changed opinions, seeing situations differently, hearing situations differently, and have become more understanding and forgiving. Taking the time to sit quietly and allow my thoughts to enter and leave as I breathe in the new breath, and release the old breath, continues to teach me the fragility and preciousness of life. I try to remember the words written by my mother "be steadfast and "gentle in thought." Meditating has become a routine practice that I look forward to with anticipation. I trust that, eventually, I will hear my truth.

As we begin to grow and to mature, we discover from living and informed study that our personal stories from our childhood influence and often determine our behaviors as adults. We come to a point in our lives where we want to find answers that will benefit our present and future biographies. It becomes very important to us to connect the intricate puzzle pieces of our lives and to emerge with a clear picture of understanding of who we were, who we are now, and who we are becoming.

Our biographies begin with our parents. My mother and my grandmother were hospitalized with scarlet fever during an epidemic in which my grandmother died. My grandfather was so bereaved that he abandoned my mother, and never saw her again.

Part of the family believed it would be best to move her to Michigan to live with cousins, but another part of the family felt she should be given an opportunity for a better life. A wealthy English couple who were looking for a daughter and a sibling for their son found the family and met my mother. At age seven my mother left everything and everyone she ever knew and was moved from a family friendly rural Pennsylvania town to a large city in upstate New York. She grew up in a wealthy home environment, but experienced a demanding, adopted mother who favored her son. Her relationship with her adopted father was a loving and close bond.

As the years passed, and after the death of her beloved adopted father, my mother's life dramatically changed. She became more of a housekeeper/caretaker than a legitimate daughter to her adopted mother. She eventually was denied the opportunity to complete her education and to take her rightful place in the same social atmosphere as her older brother.

In her early twenties, she fell in love with a young Catholic man she had met while attending university classes part time. They decided to marry, but her adopted mother refused to give them permission to marry because of his religion. When the young man asked my mother to elope with him, on a certain date at a specified time, she could not do it. She never met him, and later found out from friends, he was so bereaved that he soon accepted a marriage proposal from a wealthy, older woman he did not love.

Her decision not to meet him stemmed from her loyalty and promised commitment to her adopted father. His last request of her was to continue to take care of his wife, until her death. My mother felt she could not dishonor his request.

Many years later after the death of her adopted mother at age 96, adoption papers were searched for, and never found. My mother's inheritance from decades of loving devotion resulted in an inheritance of one diamond earring. Her older brother was bequeathed the home, and everything else. However, her true inheritance was her personal freedom, a freedom that, eventually, gave her the strength she needed to begin a happier and healthier life.

I know little of my father's background except to say his ancestry was Dutch and that he was born in this country. It is believed his father or grandfather died from the confrontation in Gettysburg. He grew up in Pennsylvania, married and had two sons. His wife died giving birth to the second son, and he found himself a young widower.

At that time, his older sister was employed as a teacher and engaged to be married. She resigned from her teaching position, and ended her engagement. She and her younger sister moved to her brother's home to raise his two sons. Although very different in physical appearance and personality, my aunts were strong, intelligent, independent women. I heard them disagreeing about politics often, each aunt holding her own view. Looking back now, those sisterly arguments were educational and enlightening to hear!

After his sons grew up and left home, my father continued to share his home and to support his sisters. He was away from home during the week, sometimes longer, as a travelling salesman for two independent calendar companies. He vacationed in Europe, and met his best friend, in Germany. They became great friends sharing music, travel, and ideas. Eventually, his friend fled Germany, and came to live in the

United States. We saw him frequently when he was in town and often shared special holidays with him. I loved him dearly as he would just pick me up, and put me on his lap while he was talking. My family was not demonstrative or affectionate physically or verbally. I was overjoyed when Uncle Ernest would pick me up, and lovingly place me on his lap.

While walking in the neighborhood one day, my father saw my mother working in the front yard of her home. He made up his mind to meet her, to court her, and to eventually ask to marry her. She met him, went out socially, found many differences between them, and did not return his love. Despite her unwillingness to marry because she did not love him, my father and my adopted grandmother made arrangements for a wedding. My mother cried in the living room. She was twenty-nine years old; my father was sixty years old.

The marriage took place and within two years I was born. From my earliest recollection, I was told by my mother that I was conceived because she had never had anything to call her own. Even though both parents were not demonstrative, I always knew they loved me. Both parents encouraged me to find fulfillment in the arts. From age 6 to age 10, my ballet and tap dancing lessons, and learning how to play the piano were happy activities for me

My favorite memories of my father are the times we would sing rounds of Row, Row, Row Your Boat on driving trips and vacations. From my father, I learned appreciation of music, responsibility to family, awareness of the world, and love of travel.

We shared a lovely, large two story home with my two aunts who lived downstairs. They showed their loving concern for me in many pleasant ways. Both aunts were interested in sharing their ideas and spending time with me. I never felt they were old and I never felt any distance or isolation because of their age. They talked with me and shared with me, always, as an adult.

When I was especially lonely, I would run down the back stairs and knock on their door, knowing it would be opened with welcoming delight. Often we would just sit and talk in the kitchen or in the living room. The radio was always playing music, except for the times when they would tune in to interviews and discussions.

I have special memories of spending time with my favorite aunt, my Aunt Lydia, in her bedroom. When I went into my Aunt Lydia's sunny bedroom with the back window overlooking a lovely, spacious, back yard full of her colorful hollyhock flowers, I always felt very happy. She would take out her jewelry box and show me her favorite pieces, telling me the history of each piece, or open a book she was currently reading and tell me about it or share with me stories about her life.

She kept a bottle of blackberry wine in her clothes closet, and every night, before she went to bed, she would pour a little glass of it, and "have a few sips to keep me warm" she told me. I never thought anything about it. In physical appearance she was very short, around 4 feet eleven inches, about 90 pounds, and frail looking with horn-rimmed glasses, but had a calming, strong aura that was peaceful to me. I, practically, skipped down the back stairs every time I could visit her and my Aunt Love. Their home was my refuge until I was almost twelve years old.

The gift that I believe I received from my Aunt Lydia was the gift of friendship. She taught me how to share and support another person. She never asked anything of me and accepted me, just as I came to her. My Aunt Love's gift to me was her insatiable curiosity about everything, and her independent mind. Both women did not have a jealous bone in their bodies.

At age seven, after walking home one day from second grade, I found my triple mirrored dresser in my bedroom, roped shut. When I asked my mother why she had roped the mirrors shut, she told me that she did not want me to grow up to be vain. I honestly do not think she realized that I was lonely. I was not allowed to have friends in our home and talked to two imaginary girls in the triple mirrored vanity dresser. I had fun making up stories with them and with me, the girl in the third mirror.

I now see the gift I was given that day. My imagination and my creativity all jumped inside me, immediately, and continue to thrive inside me today. I am thankful for this knowing presence, in addition to the added delight and joy I feel, whenever I receive even the smallest of favors. I get excited and feel very lucky for the loving thoughtfulness that brought the gift to me.

My favorite memories of my mother are the times I would see her content and happy with a radiant smile on her face. I thank my mother for giving me the gift of compassion, and an encompassing desire to stay curious and adaptive to an ever changing life. She gave me joy in creating, the love of color, the acceptance of all races, and the value of friendship.

Ellie Van Arsdale

When I was ten, my mother, after years of emotional struggle, found the courage and the strength to leave a dominant, unhappy marriage. She found a divorce lawyer she had known as a younger woman who helped her proceed with all of the necessary papers. She wanted only to take me on her new journey and settled for very little money. Over the years she had developed her sewing skills and had become proficient in dressmaking, millinery, and tailoring working part time in specialty shops to hone and define her skills. My mother, a sensitive, kind soul, held no bitterness toward my father and found strength to move on from her faith and determination to be free.

Ellie Van Arsdale

I have no temptation to feel or think discord
Or rather to think and feel it.
I have come to know that thought is the forerunner
Of all we feel, of all we do
Of all we hope to do.

Abbie May Palmer

After several years of living in a beautiful home, we left for Florida and soon found ourselves living in a very small, furnished room over a garage overlooking an alley with an unpaved road. Just before we left for Florida, I experienced my father's deep love for me when he asked me to stay with him and not go with my mother. I had to tell him that I was going to go with Mama, one of the most difficult conversations I have ever had. I did not understand my father's stern ways, but had felt his underlying concern for me. I also felt deeply, his sad acceptance of his own future. Although he drove us to Florida, I never saw or heard from him again. He passed away the following year.

The suddenness of change has taught me to live each day as the precious gift it is and to feel that I can change myself, if I remain open and willing to "accept what I cannot change." Life has taught me that it will always change. It continues to teach me that the circumstances of life can be lived with positive thought.

It has been my personal experience that the testing of a decision made to change often brings unwelcome deliveries of situations you do not want in your life. Suddenly everything goes wrong and tries to take you back to what was with a fear that nothing will ever change. And yet it always does. When we feel thwarted by a path of encounters that seem to be determined to challenge our decision, that is when we definitely know we are being tested.

Try not to be stigmatized by these situations. The testing is there because it is needed to confirm and strengthen our affirmation. Finally, after years of starting and then feeling stopped, I have awakened to the fact that my drought periods are there to show me what not to do. I have realized that I would not be where I am today if I had not been where I was yesterday. I would not be continuing to grow up. I would not be taking full responsibility for my thoughts and my actions.

The operative word here is willing. You must be willing to allow change to catapult you to a happier, stronger, and healthier you. You are the only person who is living your life. You are the one that is dealing with all of the nitty gritty. If we can make the decision to confront our negative voices, to refrain from judgment, stay in faith and listen, we will see that we are being shown our own inner strength and wisdom. Our lesson is to do the work so we can let it go and see the gift. We have to learn to face what we fear so we can actively participate in our own recovery.

When we can begin to observe ourselves and step back to take a look at our lives and our experiences, without the intense, personal, microscopic scrutiny we usually give them, we give ourselves a chance to heal. Our outlook becomes vastly more compassionate and loving

We did what we did, we said what we said, because we didn't know what we know now. Others did the same. It is time to forgive ourselves and others for holding on to past, personal experiences that have haunted us and see them as lessons in life that are igniting our spirits to reach out for healing and growth. See the gifts that were brought to you to live a compassionate, loving and generous life. See how far you have already travelled. Give gratitude to God and to your searching mind.

Ask yourself, how am I moving on? What am I doing that is positive in my life? What is it that is helping me, what is it I find joy in doing? Is it reading, taking a class, attending church, listening to music, walking in nature, caring for animals, enjoying sports, is it staying quiet and having alone time?

Where is it that I am aware of my life? Where is it that I am feeling safe? Where is it that I am feeling positive? Where is it that I am feeling healing? Where is it that I am releasing my negative past to Mother Earth and feeling joy from her willingness to take my pain? Am I letting go and letting God?

What is bringing me newly found hope and strength to savor each breath with gratitude? What am I discovering when I take the time to go inside and just listen? Where is it that I am willing to hear clearly the words that are coming to help me help myself? What do I need to make the decision that no longer will I be lazy about listening, growing, learning? What is it I can do to bring a happy word of love to someone today? Where is my patience? When will I get there?

Your determination and your will to do it will give you the strength and the energy not to give up. You can give in to what is, but you do not give up. Moving along slowly is moving along in a forward path.

My oldest granddaughter had the difficult challenge as a baby of learning how to move forward. She did not know how, could not figure it out, despite all efforts to show her, by example, how to do it. She, happily, crawled backward.

I remember getting down on all fours and coaxing her by saying "Come on, honey, just follow me. Bet you can't catch me!" hoping she would follow me. Instead, with her big, brown, luminous, mischievous eyes, she just looked right at me, and with a silly grin, a big laugh and lots of giggles, she kept crawling backward! She was happy just to be crawling, content to have arrived at the destination of crawling. Long after I returned home from my visit, I received a telephone call that all of a sudden, completely out of the blue, she had found out how to crawl forward and she was all over the house! She was still laughing, still accepting what she could do when she could do it.

When I am impatient with myself in a situation of my own, I am reminded of my granddaughter. When I feel stuck and unable to move in the direction I want to go, I realize there is nothing I can do about it except to keep on trusting, doing my work, and telling myself to be patient and positive. When I am ready I will crawl forward, be happy about my discovery, and feel thankful and joyful I am right where I need to be.

Isn't that what life is? Making our own mistakes, living out our decisions, releasing our past, moving forward in our discoveries with a new sense of hope, a renewed feeling of joy and a big smile that we are where we are now?.

Once I decided I wanted to feel happier and healthier, I started on a long path of study and self discovery. I began to change and when needed, I retired the old identity, thanking her for introducing me to my new identity. I retired her in a happy, safe, loving atmosphere, said farewell and thank you to her with love, and gave birth to my visualization, my new identity.

There are always new lessons to be learned, paths still waiting to be discovered. Like Auntie Mame, do not stop at the appetizer. Instead, continue to sample the many entrees and desserts that keep suddenly appearing in your life. Trust and believe you are a partner with God and that you are receiving newness and enlightenment, that you are listening with kinder, truer ears.

Make every day a day of loving gratitude. It is okay to be where you are today. Accept where you are and the Divine wisdom that has brought you to this moment. Continue to dream, to study, to play, to laugh, to sing, to dance, to take risks. Make a decision to be joyful. Each breath you breathe is bringing you an opportunity for new awareness to know yourself and others with loving compassion and acceptance.

Wintertime of Healing

In the calm of the air in this wintertime of healing
I see snowflakes drifting toward me
Each one floats toward me alone, yet unique in size and design
Soon surrounded by another and then another
I see you
I see me
I see all of us together, sharing our beauty
And the uniqueness of our individuality
Acknowledging it, praising it, being thankful for
The wisdom and the growth
We are continually receiving from each other
Just as we are.

Eleanor Van Arsdale

Feel the Divine love and wisdom that is yours for the asking. It is guiding you to a new identity. Open your heart to see what you need to see, to hear what you need to hear, to voice what you need to say. Above all, stay willing to trust your journey, and do your necessary work to discover your purpose. Return home to yourself and feel the warmth from your own pilot light as it guides you on your journey.

> "Therefore I say to you, whatever things you ask
> when you pray, believe
> That you receive them, and you will have them.
> And whenever you
> Stand praying, if you have anything against
> anyone, forgive him, that your Father in heaven
> may also forgive your trespasses."

Mark 11:24-25
Holy Bible
New King James Version

Wisdom comes in many forms to us throughout our lives. If we keep releasing our thoughts to this wisdom, our lives will bring us honest clarity. When we consciously breathe and quietly meditate, finding time to cherish our alone time, our inviting thoughts will magically reveal their gifts of wisdom to us. Truth will present itself as clear evidence and leave you with no doubt. In whatever way that wisdom travels to your life, always be patient and kind to yourself. It will travel to you when you are ready and will become an integral, worthy, positive addition to the kinder, wiser, more loving identity you are creating for yourself.

Our lives are lived with God's grace to us. When we take the time to re-discover ourselves, to make a definite choice to re-birth ourselves, we are reminded of how fragile life is and we begin to realize how each breath that we take in, and each breath that we give out is reminding us of our fragility. The present becomes our focus as we embrace life with more thankfulness, not taking any of it for granted.

Start listening to the breaths you take in and the breaths you release. Hear each one as the life force within you. Each breath is a miracle, an endearing gift from God. You and you alone, have the choice to create a new identity, to choose a loving, creative design to live where you are now, and where you want to be in your future.

I encourage you to make your request known, to accept the Divine guidance that is waiting for you. May you thank God each morning you awaken for each breath you have taken during the night, and for those breaths you are receiving today. Each one is bringing to you an increasing awareness and understanding. With wiser ears, eyes, mind, and heart, you are being illumined. L.I.S.T.E.N Let your inner self teach you enlightenment and newness.

ENDORSEMENTS

Carolyn Kerr's book, *Lift Up Your Head: Joy in the Face of Shame* is o
It deals with an important and difficult topic which is too often neg
in the church and in the secular world. Kerr points out how debilitati
common shame is. This is an essential work for pastors, therapists, cou
anyone who has ever been made to feel ashamed.

Rev. Dr. Paul Leg
Grace Presbyterian Church, Mo

Lift Up Your Head: Joy in the Face of Shame gives the reader unique insig
often neglected consideration of the presence of shame. Carolyn Ke
into the murky waters of the painful reality which exists for many
doing, she establishes an invaluable foundation as to the nature of
differences between shame and guilt, plus ways to overcome this highl
hazard. Dr. Kerr is particularly qualified to deal with this sticky subje
psychological education and a biblical orientation; vast cross-cultural
and years in counseling ministry. This book helps fill a void in psyc
Christian literature. It is essential reading for Christians, clergy, cou
professors in the field.

Clayton L. ("Mike") Ber
Retired president of the Latin Amer

This is a good and helpful book . . . . I am really pleased with it.

Dr. Charles H. Kraft, Seni
School of Intercultural Studies, Fuller Theologica

Carolyn Kerr has produced a valuable work on a topic which doe
much attention as it should. Since the primary cause of missionary
interpersonal difficulties, materials of this kind are extremely valuabl
societies doing member care work.

Her use of Jesus' incarnation is especially helpful. She states, "J
depend upon public opinion to know who he was." She talks about t
must have felt when he left heaven and came to earth, the terrible tr
received in general, the support he had from John the Baptist, and th
dependence on the truth and on God the Father that enabled him t
his mission. He modeled for us life and ministry free of shame.

I recommend this book to anyone struggling with this phenomen
on a personal level or as one tasked with the care of others.